B

254

THE CLARENDON BIOGRAPHIES

General Editors: C. L. MOWAT and M. R. PRICE

ISAAC NEWTON

by

J. D. North

OXFORD UNIVERSITY PRESS

1967

Oxford University Press, Ely House, London W.1

GLASGOW NEW YORK TORONTO MELBOURNE WELLINGTON
CAPE TOWN SALISBURY IBADAN NAIROBI LUSAKA ADDIS ABABA
BOMBAY CALCUTTA MADRAS KARACHI LAHORE DACCA
KUALA LUMPUR HONG KONG TOKYO

Printed in Great Britain by Richard Clay (The Chaucer Press), Ltd.,
Bungay, Suffolk

CONTENTS

LIST OF ILLUSTRATIONS

1

TWO REVOLUTIONS

WHEN Isaac Newton was born, on Christmas Day, 1642, two great revolutions were taking place, one intellectual, the other political. It is not possible to say exactly when either began, although the Civil War in England, which was the most obvious outward sign of the second, was then only a few months old. The intellectual revolution is much the harder to define, but it might be reasonable to begin with the publication of Copernicus' great work on astronomy, just under a hundred years before Newton was born.

Copernicus had revived an old Greek idea that the Sun, and not the Earth, was at the centre of the Universe. For half a century this idea was accepted, calmly enough, by a few professional astronomers, and ignored by the rest of the world. At length, however, it led to an immense intellectual ferment. Academic teaching was still the province of the Church, and it was important that astronomy, and indeed all branches of learning, should harmonize with the revealed truths of religion. When at last the conflict between the Church and the New Learning came, the Church's first tirades were not unnaturally directed at those who, like Galileo and Kepler, supported the beliefs of Copernicus. Men could say more or less what they wanted about magnetism or optics, without running the risk of offending theology; but astronomy was different. Theologians had very firm ideas about the nature of the Universe, derived in part from the Bible, but also in part from the writings of Aristotle (for whom the Earth was emphatically at the centre of things).

Galileo's life serves as a useful focal point for the intellectual revolution of the seventeenth century. The story of his relations with the Church is well known. In 1615 he was summoned before the Inquisition for disseminating opinions contrary to Holy Scripture. Proceedings were dropped on condition that he ceased to teach the doctrine that the Earth moves around the Sun. In 1632, however, he published his famous *Dialogue on the Two Chief Systems of the World*, the systems being the Copernican, and the Ptolemaic, which it was gradually replacing. It was all too evident that Galileo leaned towards the Copernican view, and again he was called before the Inquisition. This time he was both condemned to perpetual house arrest, and required to retract his opinions publicly.

There was much more to this intellectual revolution than the struggle between theology and astronomy. Galileo's *Dialogues* also suggested that Nature is uniform. Does not the same cause always give rise to the same effect? Before Galileo's time most men of learning would have admitted that in general this is so, but they would have wanted to make important reservations. For example, in common with many scientists of the present day, they wanted to exclude miracles. But they also wanted to draw a distinction for which scarcely anyone would now wish to argue, and to say that earthly happenings are of a completely different sort from happenings in the regions beyond the Moon. Had Newton believed this he could never have proposed his theory of gravitation. Gravity, for Newton, was a force which acts between *all* material objects, no matter where they may be in the Universe. It was Galileo, more than any other, who made this view tenable. How could the heavens be incorruptible and unchanging, as the Aristotelians had said, when, with the help of his telescope, he could see spots on the Sun, growing, moving, and disappearing? How was the sudden appearance of a new star, in 1604, to be explained? There seemed to be no answer to these questions.

Galileo was responsible for preaching two further revolutionary doctrines of great value to Newton. Strictly speaking, neither was new, but during the Middle Ages few people had been conscious of them. These were the doctrines that the world is essentially *mechanical*, and that it is best understood with the help of mathematics. Few would have been surprised, even before Galileo, to hear talk of 'the wheelwork of the Heavens'; but so thoroughly was the belief in a mechanical Universe pursued, that by the time of Newton's birth even the bees were being referred to as 'pretty little engines'. Two centuries were to pass before the mechanistic and mathematical view of Nature was of much value to biologists, but physics benefited almost immediately.

Why is this called an intellectual revolution? Science was now pursued with a fervour for which there was no precedent in human history. The reason was a change in mental attitudes. New kinds of knowledge could be sought, without fear of the restraining hand of tradition. This was especially true in Protestant countries, where to side with Galileo was to take a stand against the Roman Catholic Church. New insights were to be had, by the device of drawing parallels between Nature and mechanical objects whose workings were already thought to be understood. A new respect grew up for mathematics, particularly among physicists, who took it upon themselves to develop it wherever it could help them, and often where it could not. And in all these ways Newton, born in the year in which Galileo died, was a child of the revolution.

* * *

Newton's early childhood was spent in a small farm-house in the hamlet of Woolsthorpe, seven miles from Grantham in Lincolnshire. Of his father, who died before he was born, we know next to nothing. 'A wild, extravagant, and weak man,' said Isaac's stepfather, who was no doubt prejudiced. The stepfather in question was the Reverend Barnabas Smith, rector of the next parish, who married Isaac's mother two years after the death of her first husband. Mr. Smith could scarcely have been called wild himself, for it is on record that he paid one of his parishioners a fee for proposing marriage to Mrs. Newton on his behalf. As for his new wife, weakness was not one of her failings, if we are to judge by her insistence that Mr. Smith should settle on Isaac not only the income from the

Woolsthorpe farm but also land of his own worth £50 a year—a useful income in the seventeenth century.

Newton first attended two small village schools where he learned to read and write and to do a little arithmetic. At the age of twelve he moved to the King's School at Grantham, but his stepfather died shortly afterwards, and when he was nearly sixteen his mother brought him home to manage the estate. Newton's heart was not in farming. While at Grantham he had lodged with an apothecary named Clark whose brother was the mathematical usher at the King's School. The Clark family were an important influence on Newton's life, giving him an interest in chemistry and mathematics, indulging his liking for making mechanical toys, and giving him access to a useful collection of books. Childhood acquaintances later recalled his model windmill, in which a mouse played the part of miller. They remembered his paper kites, from which he hung paper lanterns at night, terrifying the country people. He made an ingenious water-clock and many sun-dials, one of which is still kept in the collection of the Royal Society. 'These fancies sometimes engrossed so much of his thoughts,' it was said, 'that he was apt to neglect his book, and dull boys were now and then put over him in form. But this made him redouble his pains to overtake them, and such was his capacity, that he could soon do it, and outstrip them when he pleased.'

In school he was given an excellent grounding in Latin, in which most scholarly books were then written, and which was still used for formal disputation in the universities. He was taught some Greek, some Hebrew, and some French, but no other modern language. He would perhaps have learned a little logic, and much Biblical history. Beyond elementary arithmetic, and such geometry as could have been found in the first book of Euclid, he does not appear to have been taught much mathematics, by modern standards. But then, much of the mathematics which is taught today is of Newton's making.

It is hard to form a picture of the young Newton's character. He seems to have been retiring, and even secretive, but not timid—it is told how he rubbed the school bully's nose on the church wall. Newton was never at ease in society. He probably never made a truly close friend, and in later life he would have suffered fewer torments had his sense of personal honour been less strong.

The Civil War must have affected his private life, although we can only guess at the extent of his family's involvement. He was only six when Charles I was executed, but political feeling ran high during most of his life, and especially during his first twenty years. His first years at Grantham coincide, more or less, with Cromwell's Protectorate. It is fairly certain that the sentiments of his family were with the Royalist cause, but later in life, with the development of his own highly personal brand of Protestantism, Newton became a Whig and an anti-Jacobite.

Newton was not a success as a farmer. He dreamed, the cattle strayed, and his mother despaired. It was decided that he should return to school to prepare for Cambridge, and after a year, when Newton was eighteen, he entered his uncle's college, Trinity. The University of Cambridge had suffered much during the Civil War. Charles I had assumed the right of appointing heads and fellows in many of the colleges, and this was in turn the cause of much Parliamentary hostility. Cambridge was a garrison town, and suffered from measures taken to fortify it, although its streets saw no fighting. Both universities contributed money to the King's cause and melted down much silver plate to pay his army, though some of the Cambridge plate was intercepted by Cromwell. Many fellows of Cambridge colleges were dismissed by Cromwell, and for years afterwards teaching was sadly disorganized. With the Restoration in 1660, although discipline was lax, the traditional routines of university life reappeared, and cannot have failed to impress the pious and diffident country youth.

Newton went to Trinity as a subsizar, that is to say, an undergraduate who paid for his tuition and board by serving, running errands, and waiting on his tutor. As a subsizar it would have been hard to lead a very riotous life, even had he wished it. In fact it is on record that he changed rooms to avoid the revels of his room-mate's companions. A good deal is known about his academic studies at Cambridge from his own note-books. His uncle is said to have given him a copy of Sanderson's *Logic*, which he studied so carefully that when he attended the college lectures he was more familiar with it than his lecturer. The story goes that the lecturer was so impressed that he invited Newton to attend readings of Kepler's *Optics*. Newton took the book home, and mastered it. When the readings began his tutor was even more astonished by his grasp of what was accounted a very difficult subject. If true, this story is the more interesting since Kepler's book was the most original work on optics then available, and clearly helped to form New-. ton's own original ideas on the subject over the next few years.

To understand Kepler's *Optics* Newton must have known some trigonometry and a considerable amount of geometry. In 1663 he is said to have bought a book on astrology at Stourbridge Fair, near Cambridge. He found that to under-stand the astronomical problems he needed a knowledge of trigonometry. An English translation of Euclid did not help him. He turned, therefore, to Descartes' *Geometry*—which treats geometry algebraically—but found himself out of his depth. Yet before long he had returned to it, and line by line worked through the book unaided.

Newton attended lectures on the Copernican system of astro-nomy, which were later to stand him in good stead. But the most important event of these early years at Cambridge was his encounter with Dr. Isaac Barrow. Barrow, only twelve years older than Newton, was a truly astonishing man. Recom-mended for the professorship of Greek while in his early twenties, he had been obliged to stand down on religious grounds—he was regarded as an Arminian, that is to say, one who flatly denied Calvin's dogma of predestination. He left England and travelled extensively, on one occasion leading the crew of his ship to victory against corsairs. After the Restor-ation he obtained his professorship, but soon resigned it in favour of a professorship of geometry at Gresham College in London—he had already produced an excellent edition of the whole of the fifteen books of Euclid's *Elements*. By 1663 he was back in Cambridge as Lucasian Professor of Mathematics, a position which he later resigned in favour of Newton himself. 'The most learned man in England,' was what Charles II called him. Had Barrow's father been alive, he would no doubt have recalled the days when he had prayed, 'God, if it please Thee to take away any of my children, I can best spare Isaac.' Restless of spirit, slovenly in dress, pale and dissipated in appearance, he smoked incessantly. Charles' courtiers could forgive him only the last of these vices, and yet they admired him for his wit, his strength, and his courage. They even forgave him his sermons. Newton, needless to say, was much influenced by this man.

After Easter term, 1663, Barrow taught Newton natural philosophy, or physics, as we should now say, which of course included optics. This last subject allowed Newton to exercise his practical skills, and fascinated him. In this, as in almost everything he studied during the years 1663-6, he was laying the foundations of his future fame. To take one example, while working on the problem of extracting mathematical roots, he was led to what is generally known as the *Binomial Theorem*. (It is given this name since it tells us how to write down the square, cube, and so on, of a sum of *two terms*.) This was an important step in the direction of the calculus, which Newton was also shortly to develop. It may be simply explained to those who are not familiar with it. Beginning with the result of squaring the expression $(a + b)$, namely $a^2 + 2ab + b^2$, and with the result of cubing $(a + b)$, that is, $a^3 + 3a^2b + 3ab^2 + b^3$, it is natural to ask whether there is any formula which will allow us to write down the result of raising $(a + b)$ to *any* power. Newton found that he could write

$$(a + b)^n = a^n + \frac{na}{1}n^{-1}b + \frac{n(n - 1)}{1 \cdot 2} a^{n-2}b^2$$
$$+ \frac{n(n - 1)(n - 2)}{1 \cdot 2 \cdot 3} a^{n-3}b^3 + \dots,$$

where the dots mean that the series is to be continued in accordance with a rule which should be obvious from the first four terms. If n is a positive whole number, the series stops after

$n + 1$ terms. If $n = 3$, for example, it should be easy to see that Newton's expression for $(a + b)^3$ agrees with that given above. (If n is *not* a positive whole number—if it is negative, or fractional, for instance—the series has no last term—it is infinite. The proof of the Binomial Theorem which Newton gave did not apply to these cases, but he knew that the extended theorem could be used, in suitable circumstances.)

*   *   *

In 1665, at the age of twenty-three, Newton took his degree of B.A., so far as is known without any distinction. The previous year Barrow had examined him and found his knowledge of geometry poor. As with many other great men, his moderate degree can be put down to his interests having strayed beyond the bounds of the curriculum. This is not of itself a mark of greatness; but it is a comforting thought that neither Newton nor Einstein excelled in formal examinations.

In 1665 the Great Plague struck the country. This was the last, and the worst, of the epidemics of bubonic plague which had depopulated the country at intervals since the Black Death of 1348. It raged from the spring of 1665 to the end of the following year. No effective medical treatment was known, and the populace lived in a permanent state of terror. Richard Baxter, for example, a Puritan preacher who had been Cromwell's friend, remarked on the way in which people 'shut their doors against their friends, and if a man passed over the fields, how one would avoid him as we did in the times of war; and how every man was a terror to another.' In the autumn, the people of Cambridge became afraid that they would suffer the fate of the inhabitants of London, where more than a tenth of the population had died in the space of three months. The university was closed, and its members returned to their homes. Newton retired to the farm at Woolsthorpe, where he lived in seclusion for nearly two years.

When he returned to Cambridge in 1667, he had made three of his most important discoveries.

2

EARLY ACHIEVEMENTS

It is unfortunate that relatively little is known of the two years Newton spent at Woolsthorpe, for this was perhaps the most important period of his life. One reason for our ignorance is the strong desire he had to work alone. He was reluctant to show his results to others. It seems to be a characteristic of mathematicians that they are averse to criticism, and Newton was certainly no exception. No doubt this goes some way to explaining why, throughout his life, he was reluctant to go into print.

Towards the end of his life, Newton referred to some of the things he wrote at this time. 'I invented the method of series and fluxions in the year 1665, improved them in the year 1666, and I still have in my custody several mathematical papers written in the years 1664, 1665, 1666, some of which happen to be dated.' In 1669 he gave a connected account of his work to Isaac Barrow, and this was circulated among a select group of mathematicians. The method of fluxions was used in mathematical problems dealing with quantities which changed (or 'flowed' as Newton often said) continuously. Newton developed his methods in connexion with some problems in geometry —such as the problem of determining tangents to curved lines, and the problem of finding the area bounded by a curve. The subject grew into what is now known as the differential and integral calculus. Later we shall see that Newton's priority in this discovery was contested. It was said by some that the German mathematician Leibniz should have been given the credit for it. Newton's protagonists claimed that the essential idea must have reached Leibniz after Barrow circulated Newton's work. On the whole, this now seems very unlikely, and Leibniz's ideas were apparently independent of Newton's, although later.

Newton's second great achievement was the invention of a new type of telescope. We have already seen his childhood capacity for practical invention. With a prism he had bought, Newton made observations on the refraction of light, a subject dealt with, to some extent, in Kepler's book on optics. Telescopes containing only lenses (in other words, *refracting* telescopes) were of course known before Newton was born. Galileo, although the invention was not his, was the first to put the telescope to scientific use. Both he, and others who had used these early refracting telescopes, had found that they had two unfortunate properties. Not only was the image of any object seen through them given a fringe of false colour, but it was also distorted in other ways. The first defect is known as *chromatic aberration*, while the most important of the remaining defects is known as *spherical aberration*. Newton later discovered the causes of both these defects, although in practice he was never able to get rid of chromatic aberration in this type of instrument. (Chester More Hall designed a lens which would do so, in about 1733. John Dollond independently exploited the idea commercially, after 1757, and made refracting telescopes which more or less eliminated chromatic aberration.)

From Greek times it had been recognized that a ray of light, on entering or leaving water or glass, is refracted. The law (usually called 'Snell's Law') relating the new direction to the old had, by Newton's time, been known for more than forty years. Ways of grinding lenses so as to get rid of spherical aberration were also known—Descartes had written much on the subject. Newton considered the practical problems involved while at Woolsthorpe. At the same time he carried out some very important experiments on the nature of white light. He came to the conclusion that even if a telescope were designed to eliminate spherical aberration, chromatic aberration would remain. His thoughts therefore turned to the curved *mirror*, as a possible replacement for one lens of the telescope.

James Gregory, a Scottish mathematician and astronomer,

and an obscure Frenchman called Cassegrain, had proposed different designs for a reflecting telescope, two or three years earlier, but neither had made such an instrument. Newton had read at least about Gregory's design, but was dissatisfied with it. He produced his own design, and from it he eventually constructed a small telescope. The arrangement of its parts is shown—(See the second page of plates, bottom.) In a letter written many years later, he said that his first telescope was only six inches long, but that it magnified forty times. The concave mirror was ground from speculum metal, an alloy of tin, arsenic, and copper. This alloy he made himself.

It was a remarkable achievement for a young man in his early twenties, and the more so because he saw quite clearly the reason for the superiority of the reflecting telescope over the refracting telescope as it was then designed. This superiority, he said, was 'the necessary consequence of some experiments which I have made concerning the nature of light'. He thought it impossible to get rid of the coloration of the image seen in a telescope made with lenses. In this he was wrong, as we have seen, and as he might possibly have realized later. The world's largest telescopes—as, for instance, those at Mount Wilson and Mount Palomar in California—are, nevertheless, *reflecting* telescopes. (The larger of these has a mirror just about 40,000 times as large as Newton's first mirror.)

What of the experiments Newton was referring to, on the nature of light? For centuries it had been realized that a beam of white light, such as the light from the Sun, was somehow changed in colour when it passed through glass or water. Scientists had puzzled over the cause of the rainbow, and even in the Middle Ages had made some headway with this problem, but the problem is much easier to discuss in terms of the passage of light through a simple geometrical object like a glass prism. Suppose that a wide beam of white light falls on a prism, and that the emerging beam falls on a screen near the prism. Only the *edges* of the image on the screen will be coloured at all obviously. (One edge will be red, the other violet. The middle will be a yellowish-white, scarcely distinguishable from sunlight.) For this reason all previous theories of the effect had been concerned only with what happened at the edges of the beam. So, for example, Descartes had said that the coloration was due to the mixing of light and dark in the region of contact of the refracted beam and the surrounding darkness. Other theories, notably those of Grimaldi and Hooke, were more subtle; but in all cases it was believed that white light was in some way *modified* by the prism, rather than split up into its constituent parts.

The modification theories were hard pressed when it came to explaining away Newton's experimental findings. These findings were explained by Newton in a letter to the Royal Society, five or six years later:

'. . . having darkened my chamber, and made a small hole in my window-slits, to let in a convenient quantity of the Sun's light, I placed my Prisme at his entrance, that it might be thereby refracted to the opposite wall. It was at first a very pleasing divertisement, to view the vivid and intense colours produced thereby; but after a while applying my self to consider them more circumspectly, I became surprised to see them in an *oblong* form; which, according to the received laws of Refraction I expected should have been circular . . .'

In short, a beam of light could hardly be merely tinted at the edges in the process of being bent, as others had supposed, for Newton had found that the beam was also spread out. As he discovered later, the coloured spectrum was about five times as long as it was broad. This broadening effect had not been obvious to Descartes, since he—like most other experimenters —had placed his screen too close to the prism. Boyle and Hooke, who were experimenting with prisms at much the same time as Newton, had in all probability seen the effect, but not its implications. Newton saw that either his experiment must be made to fit existing mathematical laws of refraction, or that new mathematical laws must be found to fit his experiment.

Before long Newton found a way of keeping the existing law

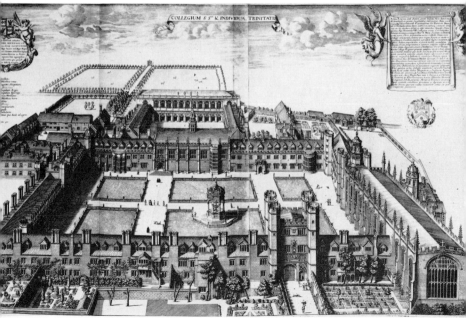

Top: Woolsthorpe Manor, Lincolnshire, where Newton's childhood was spent.

Above: Trinity College, as depicted by Loggan in the late seventeenth century. Newton's rooms were in the right foreground.

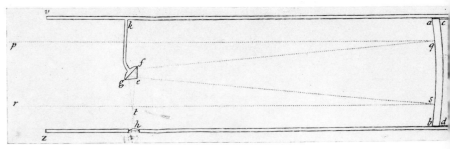

Top: Newton's telescope, in the possession of the Royal Society. Notice the eye-lens at the upper end.

Above: Newton's diagram of this telescope, taken from the *Opticks*. The mirror is labelled *ab*; *gef*, is a prism used for reflecting the rays of light from it into the eye-lens *h* (a plane mirror could be used instead of *gef*); the dotted lines are rays of light, entering from a distant object on the left.

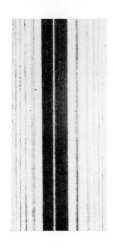

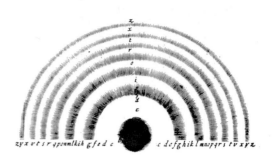

Top left: Fringes of the sort Grimaldi observed (*see page* 21).

Top right: 'Newton's rings' as illustrated in his *Opticks*.

Above: A modern photograph of the complete rings as seen in light of one colour. (The sizes of the rings change slightly with colour, and so in white light the rings, being of all colours, are somewhat blurred.)

Flamsteed's Observing Room at Greenwich.

of refraction. As then understood, Snell's Law* was applied to the beam as a whole. Newton saw that if this were done, one would not expect the beam to be spread out into a spectrum of different colours. He suggested, instead, that the law only applies to light of a single colour, and that the refractive index (which is a measure of the angle through which the incident ray is bent) is different for the different colours. White was not to be thought of as itself a colour. It was to be treated, rather, as a mixture of all colours. Each of the coloured beams falling on the surface of a refracting medium was still to obey the mathematical laws of optics. The broadening of the beam of white light, observed by Newton, was a simple consequence of the change, as between different colours, of the constant ratio (or 'refractive index') to which Snell's Law refers.

It is not clear exactly when the idea that white light was a mixture of light of many colours first occurred to Newton. Although he returned to Cambridge in 1667, once the plague had subsided, he did not announce his new theory for another two years. The idea is now a commonplace, but when first presented to the Royal Society in 1672 it stirred up a great controversy which continued well into the eighteenth century. Much of this now looks like a futile rearguard action by those who supported the modification theories of colour, but it did not seem so at the time. Newton's critics were many, but one

* This is the law which connects the angle of incidence of a ray of light (*i* in the accompanying diagram) with the angle of refraction (*r*). It states that the ratio of the sines of the angles is a constant for a particular refracting substance.

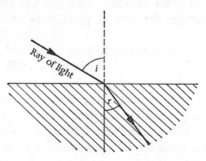

name stands out above the rest. Robert Hooke, who was Professor of Mechanics to the Royal Society, was a very talented man, but had a jealous and quarrelsome temper. He was asked by the members of the Royal Society to report on Newton's work. He admitted that the experiments themselves had been carefully performed, and even that he had himself confirmed them. He also went so far as to admit that Newton's theory was sufficient to explain the effects observed; but he thought that there were other theories—notably his own—which would do as well. In this he was wrong, but in one further criticism he was right: there was a whole range of experiments dealing with other coloration effects (as that seen, for instance, in a film of oil spilled on water) which Newton's theory could not explain. The time would come when Newton could explain these effects also. For the time being, however, he was only able to answer Hooke's criticism in part. In his reply we see something of his pride, his suspicious nature, and his fear of being criticized. On the other hand, it had hardly been tactful of Hooke to tell Newton, as in effect he did, to concentrate his efforts on improving the telescope, and to leave optical theory to more mature minds. This was not the last occasion on which Hooke and Newton crossed swords. Many years later Hooke disputed another of Newton's discoveries, almost causing Newton to omit a large part of his most famous book, the *Principia*. Hooke it was whose opposition to Newton's optical theories caused him to delay publishing his other great work, the *Opticks*, until long after he had ceased to investigate the subject. (Hooke died in 1703, and the *Opticks*, which had been in manuscript for several years, was first published in 1704.)

We have seen that Newton laid the foundations of his great work on the calculus and on optics while at Woolsthorpe. It was also during these years that he commenced work on a theory of gravitation which, as the story goes, 'he hit upon by observing an apple fall from a tree'. The story of the apple seems to come ultimately from Catherine Barton, Newton's favourite niece, who stayed with him for many years. Some historians have tried to discredit the story, but whether or not it is true—and it cannot be more than a fragment of the whole truth—manuscripts survive which show that Newton, in either 1665 or 1666, had laid down the foundations for a theory of gravitation which was almost universally acknowledged for two and a half centuries.

3

LIGHT AND ALCHEMY

WITHIN a few months of his return to Cambridge, in 1667, Newton was made a Fellow of his College. His career was helped on, above all, by Isaac Barrow, on whom he had made a great impression. Barrow's confidence in Newton was obviously not inspired by a single incident, but the following episode helps to explain why he acted as he did. Lord Brouncker had attempted to find the area under the geometrical curve known as the hyperbola. (He expressed the area as the sum of an infinite series.) In 1668 the English mathematician Nicholaus Mercator had solved the problem completely, using Brouncker's idea. The solution came to Barrow's notice, and he in turn showed it to Newton. To his astonishment, Newton produced a set of notes containing his own solution of the self-same problem. He had used a similar method, his answer having been obtained (to 52 decimal places) some time before Mercator's. At Barrow's request, Newton expanded some notes on his new 'calculus of fluxions' into an essay, which Barrow sent to an acquaintance for his comments. These were seemingly favourable. Barrow himself was in no doubt about Newton's merits, for he followed the manuscript with a letter:

'... the name of the author is Newton, a Fellow of our College, and a young man, who is only in his second year since he took the degree of Master of Arts, and who, with an unparalleled genius, has made very great progress in this branch of mathematics.'

Before long, Barrow had supported these words with deeds: wishing to return to theological studies, he resigned his professorship in favour of his pupil. At the age of twenty-six, Newton was now Lucasian Professor of Mathematics.

Newton's official duties as Lucasian Professor were not very onerous. He began his course of weekly lectures with an exposition of the theory of optics. Much of his spare time was given over to practical matters in connexion with the subject of his lectures. In particular he experimented with reflecting telescopes. One example, which was exhibited before the Royal Society in 1671, is still in the Society's possession. (See the second page of plates.) Charles II examined it, and it helped to earn Newton the position of Fellow of the Royal Society. It appears, in fact, to have been greatly esteemed, although it elicited from Hooke this claim:

'In the year 1664 I made a little tube of about an inch long to put in my fob, which performs more than any telescope of fifty feet long, made after the common manner; but the plague happening which caused my absence and the fire, whence redounded profitable employments about the city, I neglected to prosecute the same, being unwilling the glass grinders should know anything of the secret.'

This vain boast was yet another symptom of the growing hostility between the two men. Newton was perplexed, not only by Hooke's attitude, but by the refusal of most of the leading scientists of the time—in particular the Dutch mathematician Huyghens—to accept his theory of the nature of white light. He dealt with many of the objections raised, in a correspondence conducted through Henry Oldenburg, the Secretary of the Royal Society. After two or three years of controversy, his patience began to wear thin. 'I am sorry,' he wrote to Oldenburg in 1674, 'you put yourself to the trouble of transcribing Fr. Linus' conjecture, since (besides that it needs no answer) I have long since determined to concern myself no further about the promotion of philosophy.' He went on to excuse himself from addressing the Society.

One consequence of the frequent criticism of his ideas by others was that since most of his critics were followers of

Descartes, Newton treated Descartes' name with something less than fairness. (Descartes died in 1650, when Newton was only seven.) Newton owed a great deal to the famous French philosopher and mathematician, as he must have realized.

After 1675 Newton wrote nothing more on optics for the Royal Society. However, he went on experimenting with refraction, with the colours on thin films, with the nature of shadows of small objects, and with a strange and newly-discovered optical effect to be seen in crystals of Iceland spar. Above all, he puzzled over the question of the nature of light.

What *is* light? For many centuries it had been argued that a ray of light must be of the nature of a stream of tiny particles, or 'corpuscles'. Before the seventeenth century there was, in fact, only one widely-read author—namely Aristotle—who considered any other theory of the nature of light. But in the middle of the seventeenth century Franciscus Maria Grimaldi, from Bologna, made a careful study of the shadow cast by a hair. Contrary to expectation, not only did he find the shadow to be blurred at its edges, but he also discovered that when he made the illumination of the hair more intense, the shadow turned into a series of stripes, parallel to the hair (see the third page of plates). Most important of all, these stripes (or *fringes*, as they are usually called) occurred *within* the space which would previously have been regarded as the region of total shadow. The effect is known as the *diffraction* of light.

Grimaldi's observations suggested to several people that light might not be of a corpuscular nature after all. Could it, perhaps, be of the nature of a wave, a vibration in some very subtle substance or 'aether'? Water waves have the required property of bending round objects in their path, as anyone who has watched waves from a large vessel meeting a solid pier at an angle will have realized. We all know that it is possible to hear tolerably well round corners, which is another way of saying that sound does not form very definite 'shadows'. The idea that light is a vibration was brilliantly developed by several writers, notably Descartes, Huyghens, and Hooke. Newton could not agree whole-heartedly with their findings.

In his first paper to the Royal Society, mentioned in the last chapter, Newton had written up his discovery of the nature of white light in a rather odd way. 'Light,' he had said, 'is a body, and . . . as many colours or degrees as there may be, so many bodies there may be; all which compounded together would make white.' In replying to Hooke's attack, he retreated a little from his view that light is of a corpuscular nature. His discoveries, as he said, were equally well explained by supposing light to be vibrations in an aether, or even by making some other hypothesis. He was not yet familiar with Grimaldi's experiment, although he knew of it, of course, by the time he published his *Opticks* in 1704. It is not easy to trace the way in which Newton's thoughts on light changed during the last quarter of the seventeenth century. In his *Opticks*, however, he not only gives us his mature and firm opinions, but he allows himself to speculate freely, in a way which very few scientists have thought proper, either before or since Newton's time.

The first part of the *Opticks* begins by disclaiming the method of hypothesis:

'My design in this book is not to explain the properties of light by hypotheses, but to propose and prove them by reason and experiments . . .'

This echoes a famous passage in the *Principia*, first published seventeen years before. There he had written:

'. . . and I feign no hypotheses [*hypotheses non fingo*] for whatever is not deduced from the phenomena is to be called an hypothesis; and hypotheses, whether metaphysical or physical, whether of occult qualities or mechanical, have no place in experimental philosophy.'

Newton meant several different things by the word 'hypothesis'. In at least one sense of the word he *did* make use of hypotheses. So far we have encountered the hypotheses (or 'suspicions' as he called them on occasion) that light is corpuscular, and that light is a vibratory motion. Then again we saw his hypothesis that 'whiteness is a mixture of all colours'. He not only used hypotheses but he also saw that they are an essential part of science. His '*hypotheses non fingo*' was directed not against all hypotheses, but against those which were laid down with no regard for the facts. He wanted no part in reckless speculation. And like many writers since, he found it difficult to draw the line between reckless speculation and speculation of an acceptable sort.

The first book of the *Opticks* deals with the reflection and refraction of light, the formation of images and spectra, and the composition of white light. The second book was given over to the production of colours by diffraction effects, and by what we should now call 'interference effects'. If a double convex lens is placed with one surface (preferably of small curvature) in contact with a glass plate, and the point of contact is examined in white light, it is found to be filled with a series of concentric coloured rings, now called 'Newton's rings'. (Hooke, in his book *Micrographia*, 1665-7, had previously described interference effects—a rare case when his claim for priority over Newton was not exaggerated.) It is over the explanation of this kind of phenomenon, together with the diffraction effects observed by Grimaldi, that the battle between the supporters of the wave and corpuscular theories of light raged for more than a century. Newton did not adhere to the corpuscular view of light pure and simple. Instead he proposed a 'theory of fits of easy reflection and easy transmission of light'. This may be roughly explained as follows: it was said that in passing through the aether a particle of light sets up waves. These were said to move through the aether *more quickly* than the particle itself. One of the difficulties in the way of a purely corpuscular theory of light was that it was hard to see why *all* particles should not be reflected alike, when encountering the surface of, say, a glass block. We know from experience that part of the incident light passes into the glass and some is reflected. (We have all encountered conditions when it was possible to look out of a window and to see our reflection in it at the same time.) Newton's answer was that those particles will tend to pass through which arrive at the same time as the *crests* of the aether waves, while those particles will tend to be reflected which arrive with the *troughs* of the aether waves.

Admittedly, Newton preferred to speak, not of waves, but of consecutive dispositions of the medium to transmit the ray. (The interval between these he referred to as 'length of fit', and he supposed this to depend on the colour of the light in question, being greatest for red and least for violet.) In the more speculative parts of his book he tried, nevertheless, to explain his theory in terms of a straightforward wave theory.

Newton's theory explains, after a fashion, the diffraction and interference of light as seen in Grimaldi's and Hooke's experiments. Huyghens' wave theory was capable of offering a better explanation, but not until the time of Thomas Young, in the early nineteenth century, did people begin to take the wave theory seriously. It is a measure of Newton's immense prestige in England at this time that, even though Young expressed his indebtedness to Newton at almost every turn, he was attacked repeatedly for his lack of respect for the great man.

The contents of the *Opticks* were better known to the educated man of the eighteenth century than the contents of Newton's *Principia*. The latter was not only written in Latin, it was mathematically forbidding in an age which knew less of mathematics than, shall we say, our present age knows of Latin. The *Opticks*, on the other hand, was tolerably easy reading, and, strangely enough, it was through this work that many had their only first-hand encounter with Newton's thoughts on gravitation. John Locke, the philosopher, was much influenced by it, and even Wordsworth seems to have looked at it. The section which aroused most interest was the last, which comprised comments on thirty-one 'Queries'. (Only sixteen of these were in the first edition.) It is here that his thoughts on the nature of light are to be found, as well as many other scientific subjects. The Queries are framed in a curious way, almost as though Newton really believed that each should have the answer 'yes'. As an example Query 19 begins:

Doth not the refraction of light proceed from the different density of this aetherial medium in different places, the light receding always from the denser parts of the medium?'

One last word, before leaving this outline of Newton's work on optics. Despite small mistakes—he overlooked, for instance, some of the fringes to be seen in Grimaldi's experiment—Newton was a great experimenter. At the same time, he possessed a very rare gift for advancing powerful new theories, seldom allowing his theories to run far ahead of his experiments, or *vice versa*. This was one reason for his success at both.

Newton's experimental skills were much exercised in what today is usually treated as a very shady subject, namely alchemy. Although he published scarcely anything from them, it is evident from the great bulk of his alchemical notes which survive, that Newton gave much of his time to this study. An assistant, who was with him between 1685 and 1690, has left a long reminiscence of these years, of which the following is a part:

'He very rarely went to bed till two or three of the clock, sometimes not until five or six, lying about four or five hours, especially at spring and fall of the leaf, at which times he used to employ about six weeks in his elaboratory, the fire scarcely going out either night or day; he sitting up one night and I another, till he had finished his chemical experiments, in the performance of which he was the most accurate, strict, exact.'

There is no doubt that Newton seriously looked into the possibility of transmuting base metals into gold, and even sought a universal panacea, an elixir to cure illness and ensure perpetual youth. The two ideas are not as different as one might think. This was a time when many people still believed all substances to be composed of earth, water, air, and fire, in different proportions in different substances. If this were so, and if a way were found of changing the proportions, then it would be possible to change substances themselves. When it was also assumed that illness and age were the results of disturbing the true proportions of the four elements in the human body, there were obvious reasons (one might even say *scientific* reasons) for believing in the possibility of an elixir of life which would restore the true proportions, and at the same time restore health and youth. At all events, Newton shared with Boyle—the leading chemist of his day—a firm belief in these possibilities. Nowadays we tend to censure these beliefs, and accuse those who held them of having been unscientific. But the scientist is working in the dark. He is never quite sure what he will find next. Would our attitude to alchemy and astrology have been different if those who practised them had met with greater success? Their methods were often thoroughly scientific. And as for their ambitions, it is worth bearing in mind that the modern nuclear physicist is able to transmute lead into gold—at great expense, of course. One should think twice before pouring scorn indiscriminately on the darker passages of past science, or apologizing for the supposed indiscretions of such scientists as Boyle and Newton. Not all who rub shoulders with charlatans are charlatans themselves.

Boyle and Newton practised alchemy, but their work lacked the more usual nebulous and mystical overtones of the time. Boyle influenced Newton considerably, and it could be said that alchemy ended and chemistry began with these two men. Both treated the subject more as a branch of physical science than as a search for miraculous recipes. Both hoped to explain the results of their experiments in terms of the hypothesis that matter is made up of tiny corpuscles. This view, which was much in evidence in Newton's *Opticks*, was very typical of the later seventeenth century. As we have seen, this was the age of the so-called *Mechanical Philosophy*, when a common ambition was to account for the properties of bodies in terms of the size, shape, and motion of the tiny particles of which they were supposedly made. Boyle and Newton were fairly untypical in applying the idea systematically to chemistry. Boyle, for instance, explained the fact that certain substances react chemically, by saying that the particles of the one substance must correspond both in size and shape with the pores between the particles of the other substance.

Newton's great contribution to the mechanical philosophy was quite different. In fact it was not really alchemical at all. He assumed that every particle moves under the influence of every other. The idea that each body in the universe attracts, and is attracted by, the rest, underlies his monumental theory of gravitation. The idea involved *'action at a distance'*; that is to say, two objects were said to interact regardless of what lay between them. This seemed absurd to many supporters of the new mechanical philosophy. Even Newton himself had his doubts, and for many years he pondered the problem of finding a mechanism for his forces of attraction, as will be seen in a later chapter.

Newton published scarcely anything on chemistry—a 'Letter to Boyle', some of the Queries in the *Opticks*, a short note 'On the nature of Acids', and a paper, first published anonymously in 1701, on 'A Scale of Degrees of Heat'. What is now called 'Newton's Law of Cooling', well-known in physics, is to be found in this last paper. It can be counted as an essay in chemistry, however, dealing as it does with the temperatures at which mixtures of metals, in various proportions, melt. This was all highly relevant to his work at the Mint, discussed later.

Newton built no great system of chemistry, nor do we remember any great chemical discovery by his name. One or two later chemists nevertheless seem to have thought that they were influenced by him. And that, at least, is some sort of commendation.

4

THE CALCULUS

'Who invented the calculus, Newton or Leibniz?', ran a question in a recent examination for entry to the Foreign Office— and space was left for only one name in the answer. Perhaps the shortest reasonable answer is 'Both'. A more reasonable question would have been 'What is the calculus?'

In algebra we commonly use such letters as x, y, or z to denote unknown quantities with definite values. If, on the other hand, such letters can take on a whole range of different values in the course of a piece of mathematics, then they are called *variables*. So, for instance, we might say 'the variable y denotes the height of a stone above the ground, at various times'. It is possible, of course, that two variables are connected mathematically, even though the connexion is not known. If x denotes the horizontal distance of a stone from the person who threw it, we might expect there to be a relation between x and y. In fact the relation in this case may be quite simple. If x and y are measured in feet, and the stone was thrown at $45°$ with a speed of 4 feet per second, then, ignoring the resistance of the air, x and y are connected by the equation

$$y = x - 2x^2.$$

The stone moves in a curve through the air (the curve is a *parabola*), and the equation just given is called the equation of the curve. It is possible that x and y denote other sorts of quantity. A mathematical relation can often be visualized by means of a graph in the shape of a parabola, regardless of the meaning of x and y.*

The phrase 'rate of change of distance with time' is simply abbreviated in the word 'speed'. 'Rate of change of y with respect to x' is a more general idea, but it should not be difficult to grasp. For this we reserve, not a single word like 'speed', but the phrase 'derivative of y with respect to x.' (It was this quantity which Newton referred to as a 'fluxion'.) If we are talking about a graph of x against y, this derivative is occasionally called the *gradient* of the graph, just as we speak of the gradient of a hill. With a straight line graph, the gradient is constant, but with a curve like the parabola, the gradient changes as one moves along the curve. The average gradient of the curve between two points (A and B in fig. 1) is defined as the ratio $\left(\dfrac{\triangle y}{\triangle x}\right)$. As A moves nearer B, this ratio will, of

---

* Perhaps we should add that although the word 'variable' was first used for quantities which vary in *time*, like the x and y in our example, this is not an essential part of the mathematical meaning of the word.

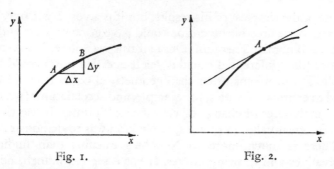

Fig. 1. Fig. 2.

course, change. When, in the limiting case, A coincides with B, it is no longer possible to draw a diagram in which $\triangle y$ and $\triangle x$ are marked in. The gradient of the curve may, however, be defined as the gradient of the *tangent* to the curve at the point. (See fig. 2.) The geometrical problem of drawing tangents to curves is equivalent to the mathematical problem of finding derivatives. It might seem that the geometrical problem is the easier to solve; but anyone who has tried to draw a tangent, even to a simple curve like a circle, without a little knowledge of geometry, will realize that the problem is not as simple as it looks. In fact, before Newton's time, there was no general rule for constructing tangents to curves, although it was known how tangents might be constructed to many special varieties of curve. What Newton achieved was to devise general rules for constructing tangents through the equations of the curves. He showed how it is possible to calculate gradients without any reference to the curves themselves. He showed, for example, that the gradient of a curve represented by the equation

$$y = x^2$$

is simply given by $2x$. (This obviously changes from one point to another, as the value of x changes.) With the help of his Binomial Theorem (see p. 11 above), he showed how, more generally, the gradient of a curve represented by the equation

$$y = x^n,$$

(where n is any definite whole number) is equal to $n \cdot x^{n-1}$. This is one of the simplest of his results, but it is a very basic one. It is hard to see how his invention could have gone very far without the Binomial Theorem. Once all this was done, Newton's theory (the 'differential calculus', as it is called now) could be applied to problems other than geometrical ones. It could be used to express velocities, for example, and accelerations (which are simply rates of change of velocities with time). It was thus of very great value in physics, as Newton was to demonstrate.

There is much more to Newton's calculus than finding derivatives and drawing curves. It has a second branch, now known as the 'integral calculus', concerned with such problems as working out areas under curves. Newton discovered that this problem is the very converse of the first—and that by and large it is a much harder problem. Briefly, if we know the derivative of y with respect to x, then it is often (though not always) possible to find y.*

By the age of twenty-two, Newton had used some of the techniques of his new-found calculus for the purposes of finding tangents, lengths of curves, and the area under a circular sector. Before long, as we saw, he had calculated the area under a hyperbola. It was after this that Barrow sent some of Newton's work to his acquaintance John Collins. Collins let it be known that the work contained some new and important results, and saw to it that several scholars perused it. It was not published until 1693, but one of those who had made notes from the manuscript version of it was Leibniz.

Was this the source of Leibniz's ideas on the calculus? Opinion is divided as to whether the manuscript (*De Analysi per Aequationes*) contains a sufficient number of hints at the direction Newton's mind was taking. The bare facts of the case are these. In 1673 Leibniz visited London and met many English

---

* For example, if the derivative were $2x$, then y could have been x^2. Actually it could have been any expression of the kind $x^2 + c$, where c is any constant number. This converse problem is called the problem of finding the *integral* (in this case, 'the integral of $2x$ with respect to x', written $\int 2x\ dx$.). Finding areas under curves requires us to be able to integrate, that is to work out integrals. Finding the lengths of geometrical curves likewise requires us to be able to perform the same kind of calculation.

mathematicians. In the following year, he corresponded with Oldenburg, the Secretary of the Royal Society, on the problem of determining lengths and areas of curves. Oldenburg hinted at Newton's discoveries, and in reply to a request from Leibniz for further information, passed on some of his results, but not the methods Newton had used to obtain them. Leibniz replied to the effect that he was engaged in other business, and was therefore unable to consider the results in the light of a 'method of great power' he had developed. Oldenburg and Collins eventually prevailed upon Newton to publish his discoveries, and in June 1676 he wrote what is now known as his *epistola prior* (first letter) to Oldenburg, asking that it be passed on to Leibniz.

In this letter Newton steered clear of his 'method of fluxions', although in it he dropped a very broad hint that he had an ace up his sleeve. In August 1676 Leibniz replied to Oldenburg, and it is evident from the reply that he was in possession of at least some results of the calculus. This prompted Newton to send his now famous *epistola posterior*. In it he described how he had devised and extended his method of infinite series. He added several theorems to his *De Analysi per Aequationes*, but was again reluctant to divulge his method of fluxions. Aware, however, that Leibniz was now a rival, and anxious, no doubt, to avoid charges of plagiarism of the sort which Hooke had previously levelled at him, he included some coded references to his discovery. (They were not in cipher, strictly speaking, but simply listed the number of occasions on which the different letters of the alphabet occurred in the latin sentences he wanted to conceal.) It seemed best, he argued, to explain his methods 'in transcribed letters, lest if others should discover the same, I should be compelled to change the method into another'. Newton's motives were nearly as obscure as his cipher.

Even had Leibniz been able to restore the complete sentences which Newton thus hid in his *epistola posterior*, he could scarcely have pieced together any more of the new calculus than he already possessed. In any case, the letter is known to have reached Leibniz at some time after March 1677, and by June of that year he had sent Oldenburg an account of his own development of the differential calculus. In this account Leibniz was open and candid, and made no effort to conceal his procedure. This was similar to Newton's in many respects, but the most obvious difference was in notation. Where Newton, for example, wrote the derivative of y with respect to x as '$\dot{y}$', Leibniz wrote $\frac{'dy'}{dx}$. (Leibniz's notation is much more convenient and is generally used today. However, English mathematicians held Newton's memory in such reverence that they persisted in using his notation—to the detriment of their work—well into the nineteenth century.)

Relations between Newton and Leibniz remained friendly for some years. At length, however, continental mathematicians tended to give Leibniz the credit for the new calculus. This fact caused much discontent among Newton's friends. In later life some of them took it upon themselves to support Newton's priority by a shameful attempt to blacken Leibniz's character. Newton at first acquiesced, and Leibniz likewise stayed aloof from the quarrel, but later each took a more active part in what was one of the longest and bitterest controversies in the history of science. Accusations of plagiarism were made on Newton's behalf, ostensibly by his friends and the Royal Society. In fact we now know that Newton himself was behind most of them.

One of the first things it was necessary to settle was the equivalence of Leibniz's calculus and Newton's method of fluxions. Leibniz and the brothers Bernoulli, for example, appear to have thought that Newton's methods were incapable of dealing with certain types of problem which could be solved by Leibniz's methods. In 1696 John Bernoulli threw out a challenge after the custom of the time 'to the most acute mathematicians of the world'. He set two problems, the harder of which was to decide what path an object should follow if it were to fall under its own weight from one point to another in the shortest possible time (the two points being neither in the

Isaac Newton, painted by Sir Godfrey Kneller.

Isaac Barrow.

Gottfried Wilhelm
Leibniz.

Edmond Halley.

Bodleian Library, Oxford

John Flamsteed.

National Portrait Gallery

Newton, as depicted on medals and coins struck in his honour
(both sides are shown).

same horizontal nor the same vertical plane). Bernoulli allowed six months for the solution to be sent to him, but received no answers. Leibniz advised him to extend the period by a year, so that French and Italian mathematicians could try as the Germans had done. Newton had two copies of the problem from France, at four o'clock of a January afternoon. His niece left this brief note on the circumstances of its solution:

'1697 Bernoulli sent problem—I.N. home at 4 p.m.—finished it by 4 a.m.'*

Leibniz, not long after, behaved very rashly. In the Leipzig journal in which Bernoulli had first published his challenge, Leibniz boasted that only those who had mastered his calculus had been equal to the task of solving the problem. And he named the two Bernoullis, de l'Hôpital, and Newton. The idea that Newton owed anything to Leibniz was very hard for Newton's compatriots to bear, and accordingly, one by one, they went into the attack. One of the most vociferous was Nicolas Fatio de Duiller, who claimed to have discovered the calculus himself in 1687, only to find that Newton had been first. In veiled terms he accused Leibniz of plagiarism. Unfortunately, it was well known that Leibniz had wounded Fatio's mathematical pride on more than one occasion. In 1704 Newton himself fanned the flames. In that year he published the *Opticks*, and bound up with the first edition of this were two mathematical tracts. His preface to the volume has this passage:

'In a letter written to Mr Leibnitz in the year 1679 . . . I mentioned a method by which I had found some general theorems about squaring curvilinear figures, or comparing them with the conic sections, or other the simplest figures with which they may be compared. And some years ago I lent out a manuscript containing such theorems, and having since met with some things copied out of it, I have on this occasion made it publick, prefixing to it an Introduction, and subjoining a Scholium concerning that method.'

* Solutions were received from two other mathematicians—Leibniz himself and de l'Hôpital. The required curve is of the type known as a cycloid. Because it is a line of quickest descent, Bernoulli named it the Brachystochrone, from the Greek *brachistos*—shortest, and *chronos*—time.

As he got older, fearing that he would lose credit for his method of fluxions, it seems that Newton lost his generosity. But Leibniz had lost his, too, and in an anonymous review of Newton's book he repaid bitterness with bitterness.

The controversy went on, mathematically uninteresting, but excellent material for students of human nature at its worst. In 1711 Leibniz, who had been a Fellow of the Royal Society almost as long as Newton, called upon it to defend him from charges of plagiarism by John Keill, Savilian Professor of Astronomy at Oxford. Unbeknown to Leibniz, however, Newton himself had guided Keill's attack: he was, moreover, now the President of the Royal Society. A committee was set up to examine the question. Despite Newton's claim that the committee was 'numerous and of different nations', it contained several of his intimate friends and only one foreign mathematician. Its report was published under the title *Commercium Epistolicum*, in 1712. The report served two purposes: for Newton, who directed the committee from behind the scenes, it was intended to be a vindication not only of his mathematical ability, but of his character. Leibniz heard later from an English friend that it was also used as a political document, by the Tories against the Whigs. Queen Anne's health was poor, and Bolingbroke's government disliked the thought of a Hanoverian succession. Newton was admittedly a Whig, but he, after all, had more than a political interest in the report. As Leibniz was Librarian to Duke George of Hanover, and also employed on diplomatic work, the Tories might well have used the report in some way to discredit the Hanoverian court.

The quarrel came to an end with Leibniz's death in 1716. In 1722 the report went into a second edition, the first being very scarce. The title-page makes no mention of any revision, and for more than a century it was assumed that the two editions were identical. However, in 1846 the English mathematician Augustus De Morgan found that several additions and changes had been made in the text, all in Newton's favour. He thought that on stylistic grounds they must have originated with Newton himself. Manuscripts in Newton's own handwriting which proved this to be so were later discovered, and Newton's immense reputation was for a time a trifle tarnished. As for the Royal Society, it came out of this very badly. Whereas individuals of both factions concerned in the dispute may perhaps be excused their impassioned behaviour, the Society, a supposedly impartial mediator, behaved very unjustly. The injustice, having been meted out in the name of justice, must have been doubly hurtful to Leibniz.

As far as the history of mathematics is concerned, too much emphasis has been put on the Leibniz–Newton quarrel. Each was indebted to a host of earlier mathematicians —Archimedes, Pascal, Descartes, Wallis, and Barrow, to name only five. It would be quite wrong to overlook the part played by these earlier writers in the development of the calculus. However, when it is a question of deciding whether Leibniz behaved dishonestly, it is instructive to recall what Newton wrote in the relatively calm atmosphere of the 1680s. He included in the *Principia* a passage which made it quite clear that he then believed that Leibniz had devised a version of the calculus, after he himself had done so, but quite independently. This passage was not included in the third edition of 1726, and it is not to be found in the English edition most often read today.

If facts like this seem to be at variance with the eulogies of those who knew Newton's fame, but not the reason for it, this is not really surprising. His character was many-sided, and if we overlook one or two monumental quarrels, he seems to have been well-enough liked. In the late 1680s, if we are to trust the word of his amanuensis, 'His carriage was . . . very meek, sedate, and humble, never seemingly angry, of profound thought, his countenance mild, pleasant and comely'. He goes on to say that (in the space of about five years) he saw Newton laugh only once. At that time Newton studied hard, took no exercise, very rarely visited others, and was rarely visited. Careless about taking regular meals, he kept very late hours, often rising after only four or five hours' sleep. 'I cannot say I ever saw him drink either wine, ale or beer,' went on the writer, 'excepting at meals, and then very sparingly. He very rarely went to dine in the hall, except on some public days, and then if he had not been minded, would go very carelessly, with shoes down at heels, stockings untied, surplice on, and his head scarcely combed.' The study of mathematics affected Newton just as surely as he affected it.

5

GRAVITATION

BETWEEN 1677 and 1683 Newton lost three good friends and found a fourth. Within these few years Barrow, Oldenburg, and Collins died. We have already seen something of Newton's debt to Barrow. Oldenburg we encountered as Secretary of the Royal Society, Newton's correspondent, and the intermediary in his encounter with Hooke. Henry Oldenburg was a German by birth, although he had been educated at Oxford. He was an avid correspondent on scientific matters who managed to hold the Royal Society together when its members treated it with indifference, financial and otherwise. Furthermore he kept up its standards at a time when it was in danger of crumbling under an attack from those who thought that it would bring about the downfall of the established religion. John Collins, who died in 1683, was one of Newton's most valuable friends. Collins was a self-educated man whose love of the sciences led him to keep up a large and lively correspondence with some of the leading thinkers of his time. He was a public servant—Secretary of the Council of Plantations—who, like many others under the Stuarts, seldom received his due salary. In the struggle to make ends meet he set up as a stationer, after which he turned to the printing of books, especially on scientific subjects. It was to Collins that Barrow had sent Newton's first work, and it was Collins who first circulated copies of it, thus making Newton's name known to an influential audience. Newton did other work for Collins, revising a well-known text on algebra, for example, and, in his turn, Collins exercised an unusual tact in eliciting works and opinions from his hypersensitive friend.

Newton's new friend was Charles Montague, a member of the family of the Earls of Manchester. Montague was nearly twenty years younger than Newton. His social position, how-ever, which entitled him to the status of Fellow-Commoner at Trinity College, brought him into Newton's circle at an early age. He was a clever young man, and an apt pupil of some of the newer ideas being introduced at this time by Newton him-self. It is difficult to obtain a true picture of Montague, for he made as many enemies as friends. He was a man of over-whelming ambition, as is evident from the somewhat absurd ode he wrote on the death of Charles II in 1685.* This earned him the notice of a great literary patron of the day, the Earl of Dorset. A later literary success—this time he was playing to the gallery—was a parody of Dryden's *The Hind and the Panther*, an attack on the English Church. (Dryden had been converted to Roman Catholicism after the accession of James II.) Montague's ambition was all too evident when, in his mid-twenties, he married his uncle's widow, the Dowager Countess of Manchester, a woman much older than himself, and the mother of nine children.

Was it ambition which led him to befriend Newton? Newton's greatness was already evident to his Cambridge acquaintances. As an intelligent member of a noble family, Montague had little difficulty in charming Newton. For New-ton seems to have yearned for social rank—witness his attempts to connect his family with the county family of Sir John Newton, to whom he signed himself 'Your affectionate kins-man and most humble servant'. He also clung to a virtually worthless title of 'Lord of the Manor', and when he was later knighted he put his signature to a pedigree which he must have

---

* The ode begins:

> 'Farewell Great Charles, Monarch of Blest Renown,
> The best Good Man that ever filled a Throne:
> Whom Nature, as her highest Pattern, wrought
> And mixt both Sexes Virtues in one Draught.'

realized was largely make-believe. Perhaps even in his generosity towards the many members of his family he saw himself in the role of head of a family of landed gentry. Newton's friendship with Montague led him, later in life, to leave the world of scholarship for the more frivolous London scene. Before he did so, however, he wrote the book for which, above all else, he is remembered, the *Principia*.

Philosophiae Naturalis Principia Mathematica, or, *The Mathematical Principles of Natural Philosophy*, was first published in 1687, a year which, for quite another reason, can be taken to mark the beginning of Newton's public life. Leaving this until the next chapter, here we shall have something to say of the contents of the *Principia*, and their sources. It is written after the style of Euclid's books on geometry, the style still roughly followed by school textbooks on geometry. It begins, for instance, with definitions—in Newton's case these are definitions of 'quantity of matter', 'quantity of motion', 'innate force', 'impressed force', and so forth. He added, 'I do not define time, space, place, and motion, as being well known to all'. He may not have given them definitions, but he devoted several pages to them, none the less. (Their meanings were also to be discussed at great length many years later, in a correspondence of a highly controversial nature between Leibniz and one of Newton's supporters, Samuel Clarke.) The *Principia* then goes on to state Newton's '*Axioms, or Laws of Motion*'. These are only three in number, but they are of the greatest importance, for Newton's entire system of mechanics is founded on them.

Law I. Every body continues in its state of rest, or of uniform motion in a straight line, unless it is compelled to change that state by forces impressed upon it.

Law II. The change of motion is proportional to the motive force impressed. It is made in the direction of the straight line in which the force is impressed.

Law III. To every action there is always opposed an equal reaction: or, the mutual actions of two bodies, each upon the other, are always equal and directly opposed.

Galileo neither stated the first, nor the second of these laws as they stand, although Newton seems to suggest that he was led to them by reading Galileo. This is surprising, for the first law is to be found in the writings of Descartes. For this reason, it is preferable to call it by its alternative title, 'the law of inertia'. The law might appear trivial, but this is not the case; indeed, it is still hard to convince the uninitiated that any object will go on moving at a constant speed unless some force acts upon it. The forces of friction and gravity are those which, in our everyday experience, are most often responsible for bringing bodies to rest.

The second law might well have been based on a law of impact framed by Huyghens, himself a follower of Descartes. It is a difficult law to comment upon. Traditionally, it has been said that by 'change of motion' Newton meant '*rate* of change of momentum' (momentum being *mass* times *velocity*). The law then simply states that the force which acts on a body is equal to the rate at which its momentum changes. It is now thought by some that in his second law, the Latin word 'vis' is not to be translated as 'force', as is usually the case elsewhere, but rather by 'impulse'. In this case, the law equates the impulse acting on an object with the change of momentum it produces. Both interpretations give the same results, in the long run. Both laws hold good in Newtonian mechanics, but not until we are sure what Newton meant can we begin to ask where he found his inspiration.

The third law is not at all obvious to most people encountering it for the first time. When I sit on a chair, it exerts an upward force equal in magnitude to my weight, acting downwards. If it exerted a greater force, I should be accelerated upwards; if a lesser force—as occasionally happens—I should be accelerated downwards. The first law tells us this much, while the second law is capable of telling us the magnitudes of the accelerations, when the forces are known. (Those who are so familiar with the third law that it seems the most obvious law in the world, may like to ponder the story of a magnet in the possession of Frederick II, the Holy Roman Emperor, which 'did not attract iron, but was drawn to it.') There are, neverthe-less, traces of the third law in the writings of both Galileo and Descartes. Newton claimed to have taken the idea from the work of Wallis, Wren, and Huygens. Why, then, do we not rename this, and indeed all of 'Newton's laws of motion'? The reason is simply that Newton was alone in selecting the wheat from the chaff, the valuable from the worthless. And there was much chaff in the seventeenth-century theory of motion. Newton took the best, he sifted it and amended it where necessary, and used it as a foundation for a system of mechanics which left all earlier systems so far behind that only the histor-ian remembers them.

Before the foundations of the system were reasonably com-plete, one further law was required. The first three laws are all very well for dealing with situations where the forces which move bodies are known, but what of the forces which keep the Moon and planets moving as they do? (We must remember that, since they do not move in straight lines, some force must act on them, according to Newton's first law.) What of the forces which cause apples to fall to the ground with constant acceleration?

Galileo had shown that objects fall to the Earth—if air resistance is ignored—with constant acceleration. Before he did so, it had been generally assumed that an object falls with constant speed, the heavier objects falling faster. Galileo showed that the weight of a falling object does not affect the way in which it falls. The story is that he dropped a cannon ball and a musket shot from the top of the leaning tower of Pisa. The fact is that the evidence for the tale is negligible, and that air resistance would have ruined the experiment; but Galileo knew that were it not for air resistance the two objects would land together. Broadly speaking, he argued indirectly from three sets of experiments. In the first he considered the times taken by a ball rolling down the groove in an inclined length of wood. In the second, he considered the paths traced out by projectiles, their ranges, and so on. In the third group of experiments he investigated the times of swing of pendulums, and the ways in which these times are related to the lengths of the pendulums. Newton's task was to reconcile Galileo's findings with the three laws of motion, and at the same time to account for the motions of the planets. He did so, with the help of his law of gravitation.

The planets move against the background of stars in a complicated way. The Sun and planets all move round a narrow band of sky, known as the Zodiac, but whereas the Sun never changes direction in its year-by-year revolution, the planets often reverse their direction. For instance, a series of photographs over a long period may show a planet tracing out a loop (see fig. 3). Many explanations have been offered for this

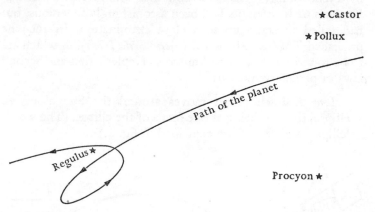

Fig. 3. A typical loop in the path of a planet, against the background of stars. (The planet Mercury followed this path during the months of July, August, and September, 1958. The only stars named are the brightest in the region.)

behaviour. Before the time of Copernicus, the most widely-accepted explanation was that made popular by the Greek astronomer Ptolemy. It was said that the planet moves round a circle, the centre of which moves round another circle. At or near the centre of this second circle was the Earth. The Earth was thus put at the centre of all planetary motions—the Sun and Moon being counted as planets. Copernicus changed this, but less than one might think. He put the Sun, rather than the Earth, at the centre of things; but the geometry of the system was much the same. That is to say, each planet moved round a circle, which itself moved round another circle.

From the point of view of the astronomer, rather than the man in the street, the really great change came with Johannes Kepler (1571–1630). Kepler was something of a mystic, and like many people before him, he was convinced that it should be possible to express the harmony and beauty of the world in simple arithmetical and geometrical relations. He spent an incredible amount of time in trying to find laws which would account for the very precise observations of the planets made by Tycho Brahe, a Danish astronomer whom Kepler assisted. Kepler's early attempts had been astonishingly ingenious, but had failed to stand up to a close examination. In 1609 he published *The New Astronomy* (*Astronomia Nova*), in which are to be found what are now known as Kepler's first and second laws of planetary motion:

Law I. Each planet moves around the Sun along an ellipse, the Sun being at one focus of the ellipse. (The words 'ellipse' and 'focus' are explained in fig. 4.)

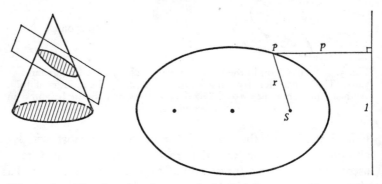

Fig. 4. An ellipse is a closed curve, obtained as the curve of intersection of a right circular cone and a plane. It is always possible to find a point (*S*) inside the ellipse and a line (*l*) outside it, such that for any point *P* on the curve, the ratio of the lengths marked *r* and *p* is constant. *S* is known as a focus of the ellipse.

Law II. A planet does not move round its ellipse uniformly, but in such a way that the line joining it to the Sun sweeps out equal areas in equal times. (See fig. 5.)

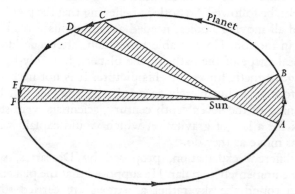

Fig. 5. According to Kepler's second law of planetary motion, if the time taken by a planet to move from *A* to *B* is the same as that from *C* to *D* and from *E* to *F*, then the shaded areas will be equal. It should now be obvious that a planet moves more quickly the nearer it is to the Sun.

In 1618, Kepler published another book, *The Harmonies of the World* (*Harmonice Mundi*), in which he stated his third law:

Law III. The square of the time each planet takes to go once round the Sun is proportional to the cube of its average distance from the Sun.

These three laws were probably the most important contribution to astronomy since the time of the Greeks. In addition, in his book of 1609, Kepler had several interesting things to say about gravity. It was traditionally held that bodies aspired, as it were, to reach the centre of the Earth. Kepler said that, on the contrary, it was the Earth which pulled bodies towards itself. If a bigger body than the Earth were placed nearby, the Earth would, in turn, be attracted by it. Gravitation was recognized to be virtually *universal*. (It is necessary to add the word 'virtually', for Kepler thought the stars were of a different nature—'ungravitational' as it were.) Kepler also saw that gravitation is *mutual*, that is to say, a stone attracts the Earth just as the Earth attracts a stone.

Kepler was ignorant of the law of inertia (Newton's First Law). Like most of those who had given the matter any thought, he followed Aristotle in believing that the planets, and indeed all moving bodies, needed a continuous force to keep them in motion. He was able to explain, after a fashion, the elliptical shape of the paths of the planets, but only by introducing magnetic forces into his picture. It is not necessary to go into details, but merely to emphasize the fact that by the beginning of the seventeenth century, scientists were starting to ask for a law of gravitation which would explain why the planets move as they do.

A different explanation, proposed by Descartes, was to become immensely popular. He supposed that the planets were carried round the sky rather as straws are carried round a whirlpool. Neither he nor his followers, however, could give a satisfactory explanation of the elliptical shape of the paths of the planets. Yet Descartes did make one very important contribution to the problem; he formulated the law of inertia upon which Newton was to base his First Law.

The next important step forward was taken by Alphonso Borelli, at about the time Newton fled the plague to Woolsthorpe. Borelli saw each planet as suspended in balance between two opposing forces. On the one hand there was the 'natural instinct' of the planet to approach the Sun. As against this, there was the tendency of each planet to fly out of its orbit at a tangent, rather as a stone flies out of a sling. (The problem here is that of calculating what are called 'centrifugal forces'.) Borelli had still not appreciated the value of Descartes' law of inertia, however, nor could he find the law governing the 'natural instinct' of the planets.

By the 1670s, most of the elements of Newton's theory of mechanics and gravitation were at hand. Huyghens had found a formula for centrifugal force in 1659, although he waited until 1673 before publishing it. Newton, it seems, had found the same formula, independently, probably in 1666. Many scientists had now come round to the view that gravitation was universal—the stars not excepted. (This is where the famous story of Newton and the apple comes in. The sight of the apple falling is said to have given Newton the idea that the Moon was subject to the *same sort* of gravitational force as the apple.) His second law of motion, which was also essential to the theory, was clear to Newton, if to no one else. One further element was needed: the law according to which the forces of attraction between objects may be calculated. This, the law of gravitation, was the touchstone of his theory, and perhaps more correctly than with any of the above-mentioned principles it may be called Newton's own. Each of the essential principles of his theory was 'in the air' at the time. Newton was faced with scores of alternative foundations on which to build. The task of deciding which were sound, and which not, was a task which could be completed only by first working out the consequences of the many alternatives, and then checking them against astronomical observations. It seems that only Newton was equal to this task.

The 'inverse square law of gravitation' may be stated as follows:

Two particles, a distance r apart, being of mass m_1 and m_2, attract one another with a force proportional to $\left(\dfrac{m_1 \times m_2}{r^2} \right)$.

(It is the square of the distance in the denominator which gives the law its name.) Here is an extract from a memorandum made by Newton towards the end of his life:

'In the same year I began to think of gravity extending to the orb of the Moon, and having found out how to estimate the force with which [a] globe revolving within a sphere presses the surface of the sphere [i.e. the centrifugal force] from Kepler's Rule of the periodical times of the Planets [Kepler's third law] . . . [I] deduced that the forces which keep the Planets in their Orbs must [vary] reciprocally as the squares of the distances from the centres about which they revolve: and thereby [I] compared the force requisite to keep the Moon in her Orb with the force of gravity at the surface of the Earth [this is where Galileo's results come in], and found them answer pretty nearly. All this was in the two plague years of

1665 and 1666, for in those days I was in the prime of my age for invention, and minded mathematics more than at any time since. What Mr Huyghens has published since about centrifugal forces I suppose he had before me.'

He goes on to say how, before 1680, he had shown that a body moving under gravity and obeying the inverse square law would follow an ellipse. The 'centre of force' (the Sun, in the case of a planet) would be at one focus. This was exactly what Kepler's laws required. The circumstances which, in 1679 or 1680, drove Newton to link Kepler's laws with the inverse square law will be explained later.

It is not entirely clear why Newton delayed so long, when he already had the inverse square law by 1666. Was it that the figures he used for the Moon's distance were so inaccurate that he put aside his calculations as dubious? Some have claimed this to be so, but it now seems unlikely. Was he simply too engrossed in other work to be able to spare the time to give this law to the world? This might have been part of the reason, but one thing seems certain: he was not sure that his law, which applied to small particles, could be extended to large bodies like the Sun, Moon, and Earth. Even if he supposed that every particle of matter attracts every other particle, it was no simple matter to work out the attraction between, say, a large body like the Earth and a particle near its surface.

Every particle in the Earth attracts the solitary particle with a force calculated by the inverse square law. The problem is to add together *all* the forces of attraction. Of course forces are not added in the same way as masses, for example, are added. The *direction* in which the forces act comes into the addition. The problem of adding up all the gravitational forces, as it presented itself to Newton, was a very difficult one. It is a problem which today is easily solved by schoolboys, using Newton's integral calculus, but it seems to have held up his own progress for twelve years or more. When he finally solved it, he found that the answer was indeed simple: the attraction of a sphere for a particle is the same as if the entire mass of the sphere were concentrated in a *single point at its centre*. In short, Newton's law of gravitation applies not only to particles, but to spherical masses. Even having solved this difficulty, it seems unlikely that Newton would have written the *Principia* without the persistence of two men Hooke and Edmond Halley, the astronomer.

Towards the end of 1679, Hooke wrote a letter to Newton in which he attempted to bury the old quarrel:

'I hope . . . that you will please to continue your former favours to the [Royal] Society by communicating what shall occur to you that is philosophical . . . For my part I shall take it as a great favour if you shall please to communicate by letter your objections against any hypothesis or opinion of mine . . .'

For almost twenty years, Hooke had been drawing together the sort of ideas discussed in this chapter. He knew nothing, of course, of the use to which Newton had put the inverse square law, but, as we shall see, it had already occurred to him that the law of gravitation was indeed a law of inverse squares. He now went on in his letter to ask Newton to consider a certain hypothesis of his own invention, relating to the paths of planets. Newton, in his reply, pointed out, rather tactlessly, that he had never heard of Hooke's hypothesis. As to the problem of planetary orbits, he evaded the issue. Instead, he added a small morsel of his own making: he argued that a falling object would *spiral* as it fell towards the Earth's centre. Hooke responded by finding a small fault in Newton's working—a fault which he announced proudly to the Royal Society. The battle was on once more.

In his next reply to Newton, Hooke actually proposed, in a veiled way, the inverse square law of gravitation. He outlined a use for the law which shows that, left to Hooke, it would never have attained the status of anything more than an inspired guess. Newton never answered the letter, but at last he had a clear-cut problem to work on. Is the law of force which leads to a prediction of elliptical orbits an inverse square law? We have already seen the answer, which Newton had certainly found before 1683 and probably before 1680.

In 1684, Halley and Hooke met Sir Christopher Wren—a first-class mathematician as well as an architect—to discuss the whole question of gravitation. Hooke maintained that he was able to prove that the movements of the planets followed from the inverse square law. Wren was obviously doubtful, for he offered the present of a book costing forty shillings to either of the others if they could bring him the proof within two months. 'Mr Hooke then said that he had it,' wrote Halley, 'but he would conceal it for some time, that others trying and failing might know how to value it, when he should make it public.' He went on to say that, even so, 'Sir Christopher Wren was little satisfied that he could do it.'

Halley tried the problem in vain. The following August he set out for Cambridge to get Newton's views. In the words of John Conduitt (husband of Newton's favourite niece, and a member of his household for the last ten years of his life), Halley asked Newton:

'. . . what would be the curve described by the planets on the supposition that gravity diminished as the square of the distance. Newton immediately answered, *an ellipse*. Struck with joy and amazement, Halley asked him how he knew it? Why, replied he, I have calculated it; and being asked for the calculation, he could not find it, but promised to send it to him.'

These are the circumstances under which the *Principia* came to be written. Newton's mathematical knowledge was now immeasurably greater than in the days at Woolsthorpe, when he had taken the first faltering steps towards a theory of gravitation. He now set to work, and wrote down his principles of mechanics in a little book *On the Movements of Bodies* (*De Motu Corporum*), which later served as a course of nine lectures. On sending his proofs to Halley, he was urged to send an abstract to the Royal Society, to establish priority. Halley also pressed him to publish his findings, and in 1685 the task was begun. Written in Latin, the language of the learned world of the seventeenth century, it took about eighteen months to complete. As explained at the beginning of this chapter, it is an austere book, written in the manner of a geometrical text. Since the major part of it was completely and utterly new, the geometrical style no doubt helped Newton to organize his thoughts. It is something of a surprise to find that he does not seem to make much use of his calculus in the *Principia*. It seems that he used it to obtain many of his results, only to rewrite the proofs afterwards in a traditional geometrical style.

Who was to pay for publication? The finances of the Royal Society had been much upset by their having published a book on fishes, very few copies of which were sold. Halley decided to undertake the business of seeing the *Principia* through the press, and paying for the printing. Not only did he do this, but he corrected the proofs, checked the calculations, and worked with the printers himself. He wrote tactful letters to Newton, who was once again the object of Hooke's wrath. At first Hooke merely asked for some sort of acknowledgement. He had no idea that Newton had arrived at the inverse square law long before his letter suggesting the self-same law. A generous word would have cost Newton nothing, but he lost his temper. In a letter to Halley, he threatened to keep back the third book of the *Principia* ('On the system of the world'). 'Philosophy,' he wrote (or 'science', as we should say), 'is such an impertinently litigious lady, that a man had as good be engaged in lawsuits, as have to do with her. I found it so formerly, and now I am no sooner come near her again, but she gives me warning.' Halley calmed Newton down, and persuaded him, eventually, to publish Book Three. In 1687, near midsummer, Halley's efforts bore fruit. What might very well be called the greatest scientific work ever written, at last saw the light of day.

This was a difficult book for mathematicians to understand. There was only one review of it, at the time, and that was written by Halley, whose financial interest in the book was not inconsiderable! Unbound, the book sold to booksellers at six shillings (or five shillings, ready money). Recently, a copy of the original edition fetched more than £3,000.

So important an occasion was the publication of the *Principia* recognized to be, that a special meeting was arranged at which James II was presented with a copy. Halley drew up a paper with a simple outline of the book, and a letter, offering his services if there was anything in it his monarch could not understand. If Halley was looking for financial assistance, he did not receive it. The year was 1687 and James's mind was elsewhere; indeed, as far as science was concerned, it had always been elsewhere. For a brief spell, however, his mind was very much on Newton and his university, and for an entirely different reason, as we shall shortly see.

To describe the fate of the *Principia* would be to recount most of the history of the physical sciences from the middle of the eighteenth century to our own time. Admittedly the best part of thirty years passed by before the leading mathematicians of the age had mastered the book, and nearly twice as long before it was much used in the universities. The Scottish universities seem to have found its worth before the two English ones. Strangely enough, its introduction to the Continent was as much due to Voltaire as to any mathematician. Voltaire was converted during a stay in England (1726–9), and on his return to France wrote tracts pointing to the advantages of Newton's system over that of Descartes. Thus goaded into reading the *Principia*, continental mathematicians exploited it far more effectively than Newton's countrymen were to do for many years. In part this was because English mathematicians stuck to Newton's notation in the calculus, rather than Leibniz's. As has been said, this is much the easier to use, and is the one generally used today.

It was the French mathematicians Lagrange, Laplace, and D'Alembert, together with the Swiss, Euler, who took Newton's work to its greatest heights. By the time Laplace had written his *Mécanique céleste*, in thirteen compendious volumes, scientists had become accustomed to the idea that the universe is a huge machine, inexorably guided by Newton's laws. ('Where does God come into your system?' asked Napoleon of Laplace. 'I have no need of *that* hypothesis, sire,' came the reply. Newton, who had tried desperately to bring God into the *Principia*, would have been very hurt.*) In the nine-

* There, after discussing God's nature, he finished by claiming that we know Him 'only by His most wise and excellent contrivances of things, and final causes'. 'And thus much,' he added, 'concerning God; to discourse of Whom from the appearances of things, does certainly belong to Natural Philosophy.'

teenth century, when many new sciences were developed, the idea of a machine-like universe persisted. Perhaps the greatest tribute to Newton's theory of mechanics and gravitation is that, where possible, the newly emerging sciences were modelled upon it.

6

A MAN OF AFFAIRS

LONG before his accession to the throne, it had been the ambition of James II to re-establish the Roman Catholic faith in England. It was natural enough that the small band of Jesuits advising James should look upon the universities with some apprehension. They were of overwhelming importance in filling high offices in Church and State. Why not turn the colleges into Catholic seminaries? James first moved against Oxford, but with very limited success. In Cambridge he tried to achieve his ends by ordering that a Benedictine be admitted to the degree of Master of Arts without taking the customary oath. The university resisted, and at length the Court of High Commission summoned the Vice-Chancellor and Senate to appear before Judge Jeffreys, who presided over the lately re-established Court. Newton was one of the nine men who eventually represented the university's cause. They left, after an ignominious hearing, with Jeffreys admonishing them: 'Go your way and sin no more lest a worse thing befall you'; but the King became uneasy, seeing the opposition he had stirred up, and withdrew his order. Although Newton remained silent throughout the official proceedings, we know that when all the other delegates were prepared to capitulate, Newton persuaded them to stand firm. He appears to have been more afraid of Roman Catholicism than many of his countrymen. At all events, they owed to him, as much as anyone, this small victory over the ill-advised James. In 1688 the university, remembering

Newton's part in this affair, elected him as their representative to the Convention Parliament. This point marks a great change in Newton's life. Until then he had been first and foremost a scholar. His social affairs had been conducted on a small scale. He was in his late forties, exhausted by the immense amount of effort he had put into writing the *Principia*. Now he was thrust into the world.

At first Newton was content to watch the world go by. It is said that his only speech in Parliament was to ask an usher to close a window. He renewed his acquaintance with Montague, whose fortunes as a parliamentarian were rising fast. At the Royal Society he encountered Hooke, who had never forgiven him his supposed injustice over the law of gravitation, and another London acquaintance was the philosopher John Locke, for whom Newton prepared a simplified version of the chief results of the *Principia*. After a few months he had to return to Cambridge. The Whigs had pursued their policies with rather too much fervour, and a newly-elected House contained a Tory majority. In Cambridge, Newton's thoughts turned for a while to theology, and he produced his most important work on that subject: *Two Notable Corruptions of Scripture*. This was a very daring essay in which he challenged the authenticity of the two passages in the New Testament on which the doctrine of the Trinity rests (First Epistle of John, ⅴ verses 7 and 8; and First Epistle to Timothy III. 16). He also gave much thought to the prophecies of the Book of Daniel, and the Apocalypse. (It was customary to find there dire warnings of the supposed iniquities of the Church of Rome to come.)

But Newton had tasted public life, and now wanted more of it. Powerful as his friends in London were, for a time they could not obtain an appointment for him. He hoped that Locke might obtain for him the post of Comptroller of the Mint, but nothing came of this, for the time being, and he thought little of an alternative suggestion that he take the Mastership of Charterhouse.

In 1691 there died one of England's leading men of science,

Robert Boyle. Boyle believed that in discovering scientific laws, man was providing evidence for God's providence. In his will, he established an annual lecture for 'the defence of religion against infidels'. The first Boyle lecturer was a brilliant young scholar of thirty, Richard Bentley. Under the title *A Confutation of Atheism*, he spoke on the theme that Divine Providence was evident to any who could perceive the grand design of the universe, as revealed by Newton. The lectures, which were given in 1692 from the pulpit of St Martin-in-the-Fields, in London, were the first occasion on which Newton's name was brought before a large section of the general public. Before Bentley published his lectures, he corresponded with Newton to make sure that he had not seriously misunderstood Newton's intentions. This correspondence gave Newton a chance to consider the philosophical consequences of some of his scientific ideas. Bentley unwittingly set a fashion, which persisted for a century and more, for deducing religious truths from the equations of the *Principia*. It is not clear from the correspondence whether Bentley ever understood all Newton's intentions properly—he certainly never understood his mathematics, but his lectures brought him fame.

At about this time, Newton began to complain of loneliness, and of several minor ailments. He began to suspect his friends of conspiring against him to prevent his obtaining public office. His lack of success preyed on his thoughts, and it was widely believed at the time that his mind had become deranged, either from working too hard, or, as some said, from the loss by fire of his laboratory and papers. Whatever the reason, there are letters to Pepys and Locke which are clearly the work of a deluded mind. A letter to Locke of September, 1693, begins:

'Being of opinion that you endeavoured to embroil me with women and by other means, I was so much affected with it, as that when one told me that you were sickly and would not live, I answered 'twere better if you were dead. I desire you to forgive me this uncharitableness.'

There is much pathos in this and his later correspondence.

We have already seen something of Newton's genius for

arousing, and taking part in, controversy. One more great dispute must be added to the list. From around 1694 until the end of the century, Newton worked at the problem of accurately explaining the motion of the Moon. (It would have been immensely helpful to navigators, if they could have been given tables predicting the Moon's position.) It was essential that Newton be given the best possible astronomical observations for his task. The leading astronomer of the time was John Flamsteed, the Astronomer Royal. Flamsteed was by nature irritable and proud, and it now seems inevitable that he and Newton should have quarrelled. His irritability had many causes. Although Astronomer Royal, he was inadequately paid. Royal patronage stopped short at his title and the buildings associated with it. He had to borrow instruments and beg for private funds to buy more, and was forced to eke out his income by giving private tuition and acting as parish priest. As a result, his health suffered. He was tormented by frequent headaches and indigestion, but he set himself an impossibly heavy programme of star cataloguing. And now Newton was making inordinate demands on his time.

Flamsteed had immediately sent Newton all the results of the observations he had made of the Moon's positions. As Newton's requests for further observations continued, Flamsteed sent more and more measurements. Newton's impatience, however, occasionally got the better of him, and some of his letters have very peevish overtones. What is more, he broke faith with Flamsteed in showing some of his work to his rival Halley. At the end of all this, Newton left his theory of the Moon's motion in an unfinished state. The fault, if fault there was, can hardly have been Flamsteed's. Newton's early biographers nevertheless attacked Flamsteed's reputation with great venom. Although Flamsteed had a very quick temper, throughout the correspondence with Newton he kept it in check—even to the point of retaining a letter and toning it down a few days later. Newton handled him without tact, offering him money for his services, and scorning his assistance in the calculations. In the end he became angry with Flamsteed for delays in forwarding observations, and complained to others that Flamsteed was holding up the theory of the Moon's motion. He wrote an unpleasant letter to Flamsteed, who, considering the circumstances, sent a most generous reply to the effect that Newton's theoretical contribution was of much greater value than his own observations, 'as the wire is of more worth than the gold from which it is drawn'. 'I gathered the gold matter,' he went on, 'and fined and presented it to you sometimes washed. I hope you value not my pains because they became yours so easily.' A man with greater understanding of human nature than Newton possessed could have taken this opportunity of patching up the quarrel. He scarcely seems to have tried. For a time the two men's paths separated. Flamsteed went back to gathering gold for his own purposes. Newton, however, turned aside from metaphorical gold. In 1696 he was made Warden of the Mint.

The Whigs had been returned to office, and Montague was at last in a position to reward his old friend. Montague's ambition—and achievement—was to bring about a series of important financial reforms. (He founded the Bank of England, and floated the national debt, for instance.) A vital part of this task involved a complete recoinage. Although a milled edge had been introduced at the time of the Restoration, to prevent the clipping of coins, the old coinage continued in use. In 1695 it was found that the average value of a silver shilling had been halved over the years by clipping. Trading was thus in a state of chaos. Buying and selling goods involved not only fixing a price, but putting a value on the coins to be exchanged. Now Montague had persuaded Parliament to pass a Bill which stipulated that after 4 May 1696, it would be illegal to pass clipped coin. The amount of work and planning involved in the necessary recoinage was prodigious. Under Newton's direction, the weekly coinage minted rose to something like a hundred and twenty pounds weight. Not until 1699 was the recoinage completed. Newton was given the title of Master of the Mint, and an income of over two thousand pounds a year. He seems to have turned away as much again in gifts and

bribes. The flow to the gallows of counterfeiters and mutilators of coin was much reduced. (However, Newton's opinion on a counterfeiter convicted after the recoinage was: '. . . it's better to let him suffer, than to venture his going on to counterfeit the coin and teach others to do so until he can be convicted again, for these people very seldom leave off. And it's difficult to detect them.')

While living in London, his niece, Catherine Barton, managed his house. She became the toast of a famous Whig club, the Kit-Cat club, of which Montague was a member. There is no doubt that Montague fell in love with Miss Barton, and that she lived in his house, either as his mistress or as his wife. (Voltaire might have been wrong, but he was probably echoing a well-known scandal when he said of Newton's appointment to the Mint: 'The infinitesimal calculus and gravitation would have been of no assistance to him without a pretty niece.') When Montague, now Lord Halifax, died in 1715 he left Catherine Barton a large legacy. Two years later she married John Conduitt, and together they lived in Newton's house until he died. Conduitt was then himself given Newton's post at the Mint.

In 1698 came the final break with Flamsteed. Flamsteed was anxious that the large sums of money spent by the King, the nation, and himself, should be justified in the eyes of the world. He wished to publish some of his observations. Newton, on the other hand, was afraid that the world might expect too much of his lunar theory—which was far from complete. 'I do not love to be printed upon every occasion', he wrote to Flamsteed, 'much less to be dunned and teased by foreigners about mathematical things, or to be thought by our own people to be trifling away my time about them, when I should be about the king's business.' Flamsteed was deeply hurt. He pointed out that Newton had not thought his work trifling when living in Cambridge. The men continued to meet, but any friendship was now at an end. From cold mutual regard their relations turned into active hostility. Flamsteed's great work, *Historia Coelestis Britannica*, was to be published, and Prince George of

Denmark was persuaded to finance it. Without Flamsteed being consulted, referees were appointed to supervise the work, and they included Wren and Newton. Flamsteed, lacking the necessary money, was forced to accept. In 1708 the referees told him that if he did not show more enthusiasm for the work, someone else would be employed to correct it. Flamsteed protested to Wren, but the only effect of this was to make Newton adamant. When Prince George died, his money was returned, and with only the first volume published, work was suspended.

Newton's behaviour at this time can only be described as vindictive. Obtaining another financial grant, from Queen Anne, he took the opportunity of having a Board of Visitors appointed to the Royal Observatory. The Observatory was virtually the creation of Flamsteed, and now he was to be at the beck and call of a committee directed by Newton himself. In 1711, Newton ordered Flamsteed to attend a meeting to decide whether his instruments were in a fit state to carry out astronomical observations. All pretence of civility was abandoned. By 1716 Flamsteed was sending attorneys to Newton, without success, to recover his manuscripts. And when Newton published the second edition of the *Principia*, Flamsteed's name was erased almost throughout.

Flamsteed would no longer act as editor of his own work, and his rival Halley took over his duties. After its publication, however, Flamsteed managed to get hold of 300 out of the edition of 400 copies. He burnt them 'that none might remain to show the ingratitude of two of his countrymen'. An edition was eventually produced under his own guidance, and appeared six years after his death.

Once the recoinage was complete, Newton's post became something of a sinecure. He had sufficient leisure to write the *Opticks*, enter into controversy with Leibniz, and produce his minor works on heat and chemistry. Honours were showered on him. He was made a Foreign Associate of the French Academy of Sciences in 1699. When Hooke died in 1703, Newton was made President of the Royal Society, to be re-elected annually until his death. He did not invariably manage to keep awake at its

meetings; but he was, after all, eighty-five when he died. For a
short period he was again a Member of Parliament, and in 1705
he was knighted by Queen Anne, who held court in his old
college for the ceremony. If the knighthood was conferred for
scientific merit this was the first occasion in English history,
and the last for three quarters of a century.

Newton wrote a great deal on religious subjects. He was
recognized as one of the most learned Biblical critics of his day,
although many of his friends feared he was guilty of heresy.
Another pursuit of the latter half of his life was one he had
followed from his youth: the compilation of a chronology of
ancient times. He prepared a manuscript on the subject for the
Princess Caroline, daughter of George I. To his annoyance, a
French translation was published without his consent, and this
became the subject of yet more controversies, which dogged
him to the end of his life. His health declined steadily for three
or four years, and he died on 20 March, 1727. He was buried in
Westminster Abbey, with greater honours than had ever been
accorded to an Englishman not of royal blood.

In his personal character, as might be expected, Newton was
often depicted as the eccentric and absent-minded scholar,
totally absorbed in his private thoughts. Did he really lead his
horse up a hill, as a boy, only to find, when he reached the top,
that he had the bridle in his hand, but no horse? Was he really
goaded into proposing marriage to a lady, only to use her little
finger, absent-mindedly, to tamp his pipe? Did he really cut two
holes in his door at college, a large one for his cat, and a smaller
one for her kitten? There is no doubt that he had great powers
of concentration, and that he was able to close his mind to all
but immediate problems, but he had his share of worldly
wisdom, even so. Despite losing £9,000 or more in the South
Sea Bubble, he managed his affairs so adroitly as to leave a
fortune of over £30,000. His life in London opened up some of
the crevices of his mind, but he never cultivated the arts, if we
exclude mathematics. He only once attended the opera, saying
of it afterwards: 'There was too much of a good thing, 'twas

like a surfeit of dinner. The first act I heard with pleasure, the second stretched my patience; at the third, I ran away.'

In appearance Newton was rather short, but with a good physique and of great vitality. In portraits, he is usually seen with his wig, after the manner of the times. His own hair is said to have been white from his early thirties. Accounts of his demeanour vary: according to some, he had a languid look, according to others, a piercing eye. In his portraits his countenance varies from one of benevolence to one of mild hostility. This is no contradiction: we have seen how variable was his character. On the whole he was remembered more for his kindness than for his spite. But the poet Cowper can hardly have been aware of Newton's relations with Hooke, Leibniz, and Flamsteed, when he wrote:

> 'Patient of contradiction as a child,
> Affable, humble, diffident and mild,
> Such was Sir Isaac.'

Flamsteed's judgement was that he was prone to flattery. We know that he found it hard to bear criticism, but we also know that his critics were wrong more often than they were right.

What of his incomparable achievements in mathematics and science? Lagrange may have been right to claim that 'Newton was the greatest genius that ever existed', but he was misguided when he went on to say that Newton was the most fortunate, there being only one universe whose laws were to be discovered. The laws of science are always open to change. Even Newton's greatest scientific achievement, his theory of gravitation is known to be only partially satisfactory. Einstein has provided us with a new theory in its place. But as Einstein frequently remarked, his own theory of gravitation rested on foundations laid down by Newton. There is no end to scientific change, and, ultimately, great scientists are judged in the same way as we judge great revolutionaries. We ask by how much they changed the *status quo*, and with what result. Even in mathematics, where truths are of a more lasting kind, fashions change from one age to the next. Great mathematicians are, in the last resort, ignored rather than proved wrong. But by ignoring a man, one cannot take away the part he played in history. Newton's part was such that it is extremely difficult to envisage what sort of place the world would have been without him—in either a material or an intellectual sense. Yet his own perspective was very different from ours. At the end of his life, he made this comment:

'I do not know what I may appear to the world; but to myself I seem to have been only like a boy, playing on the sea-shore, and diverting myself in now and then finding a smoother pebble or a prettier shell than ordinary, whilst the great ocean of truth lay all undiscovered before me.'

NOTES ON FURTHER READING

For the background to Newton's scientific work, the middle chapters of H. Butterfield's *The Origins of Modern Science* (London, 1958) make easy reading. There are, of course, many other excellent books covering the same period, and most libraries will have one or two.

The best way to appreciate Newton is to read a modern edition of something he wrote. The *Opticks* is probably the easiest of his works to read, and is available in a paperback edition (Dover). The *Principia* is sterner stuff, but worth attempting. Many of his other writings are readily obtainable, for example: his theological manuscripts (ed. H. McLachlan, 1950); his papers and letters on natural philosophy (ed. I. B. Cohen, 1958); much of his correspondence (ed. H. W. Turnbull, 1959, in progress), some unpublished scientific papers (ed. A. R. and M. B. Hall, 1962), and mathematical works (ed. D. T. Whiteside, 1964, in progress).

The personal details of Newton's life are profusely and accurately set out in L. T. More's *Isaac Newton* (New York, 1934 and paperback). Many of the collections already mentioned have good historical commentaries. Many school libraries will have *The Mathematical Discoveries of Newton* (London, 1954) by H. W. Turnbull. Unfortunately, there is still no truly scientific biography of a comprehensive sort. The older biographies by J. B. Biot (1829) and A. De Morgan (1914, written much earlier) should be read cautiously. This applies even more to Sir David Brewster's books on Newton, which are good examples of the heroic style of biography of the last century.

Newton at the Mint (1946), by Sir John Craig, is an entertaining account of the last part of Newton's life. And finally, a title which speaks for itself, *Newton demands the Muse: Newton's Opticks and the Eighteenth Century Poets* (Princeton, 1946, 1963) by M. H. Nicolson.

AN OUTLINE OF NEWTON'S CAREER

(Titles of books, and events of national importance, are printed in italics.)

1642   *Outbreak of civil war in England.* Death of Galileo.
       (Christmas Day) Isaac Newton born at Woolsthorpe, Lincolnshire.

1646   Leibniz born.

1648   *Second Civil War. End of the Thirty Years War in Europe.*

1649   *Execution of Charles I.*

1654   *Cromwell made Protector.*

1658   *Death of Cromwell.*

1660   *Restoration of the Monarchy. Charles II. Royal Society founded.*
       (June 5) Newton enters Cambridge as subsizar at Trinity College.

1664   *Second Dutch War.* Boyle's *Experiments and Considerations Touching Colours.* Newton a Scholar of Trinity.

1665   *The Great Plague.* Newton leaves Cambridge for Woolsthorpe.

1667   (Feb. 12) Returns to Cambridge. (July) M.A. and Fellow of Trinity College.

1669   Lectures in optics. (Oct. 29) Lucasian Professor.

1671   Newton exhibits to the Royal Society.

1672   *Third Dutch War.* (Jan. 11) Newton elected to Royal Society. His first paper published by that society.

1673   *Test Act.* Leibniz's letters to Oldenburg.

1676   Newton's *Epistola Prior* to Oldenburg (June 13) and *Epistola Posterior* (Oct. 24). Correspondence with Hooke.

1677   Death of Barrow.

1678   Death of Oldenburg. Grew and Hooke become joint Secretaries.

1679   Further correspondence with Hooke. Letters to Boyle. First meeting with Montague.

1681   Correspondence with Flamsteed.

1684   Discussion of gravitation, between Wren, Hooke, and Halley.
       Leibniz's first publications on the calculus.
       De Motu Corporum. Newton begins the *Principia.*

1685   *Accession of James II.*

1687   Court of Ecclesiastical Commission. Newton's defence of his university. First edition of the *Principia.*

1688   *Abdication of James II.*
1689   Newton takes seat in the Commons.
      Accession of William and Mary.
1690   *Two Notable Corruptions of Scripture,* and another religious paper (in French).
1691   Death of Boyle.
      Beginning of another long correspondence with Flamsteed.
      Period of mental breakdown begins.
1692   Letters of Bentley. Bentley's *Confutation of Atheism.*
1694   *Death of Mary II.*
1696   Newton made Warden of the Mint.
1699   Newton made Master of the Mint. Elected to the French Academy. Papers on heat.
1701   Newton again chosen for Parliament. Resigns Professorship and Fellowship.
1702   *Accession of Queen Anne.*
1703   Newton President of the Royal Society. Death of Hooke.
1704   First edition of the *Opticks.*
1705   Newton knighted by Queen Anne.
1707   First volume of Flamsteed's *Historia Coelestis.*
1708   Death of Prince George of Denmark.
      Beginnings of the fluxions controversy.
1712   Royal Society committee to investigate fluxions. Flamsteed's work published with Halley as editor.
1713   Second edition of the *Principia.*
1714   *Accession of George I.*
1715   Death of Montague.
      Correspondence between Leibniz and Clarke begins.
1716   Death of Cotes and Leibniz.
1717   Second edition of the *Opticks.*
      Catherine Barton marries Conduitt.
1719   *South Sea Bubble.* Death of Flamsteed.
1721   Third edition of the *Opticks.*
1723   Newton begins work on the third edition of the *Principia.* His health begins to deteriorate.
      Flamsteed's own edition of his *Historia Coelestis,* posthumously published.
1726   Third edition of the *Principia.*
1727   (March 20) Death of Newton.

1730   Fourth edition of the *Opticks,* 'corrected by the author's own hand'.
1776   Samuel Horsley proposed publication of Newton's works, and five volumes followed at intervals.

INDEX